Granville Sharp

## A Short Treatise on the English Tongue

Being an attempt to render the reading and pronunciation of the same

more easy to foreigners

Granville Sharp

**A Short Treatise on the English Tongue**
*Being an attempt to render the reading and pronunciation of the same more easy to foreigners*

ISBN/EAN: 9783337393366

Printed in Europe, USA, Canada, Australia, Japan

Cover: Foto ©Paul-Georg Meister /pixelio.de

More available books at **www.hansebooks.com**

# A SHORT TREATISE

## ON THE

## ENGLISH TONGUE.

Being an Attempt to render the

## Reading and Pronunciation

OF THE SAME

More EASY to FOREIGNERS.

---

LONDON:

Printed for R. HORSFIELD in Ludgate Street, and I. ALLIX in Glanville Street, Rathbone Place.

MDCCLXVII.

# INTRODUCTION.

IT is generally allowed, that the moſt eaſy method of attaining any living language is to aſſociate and converſe with thoſe who ſpeak it. Neverthelefs, when a foreigner has by this means ſo far acquired the Engliſh tongue, that he ſhall be able to ſpeak it, and under-ſtand it when ſpoken, tolerably well, he will yet find himſelf greatly at a loſs, when he at-tempts to read : becauſe the manner of ex-preſſing ſounds by letters in his own language is ſo very different from ours, that many Engliſh words, which he is well acquainted with by ear, will not appear to him to be the ſame when he ſees them in writing.—For not only various ſounds are expreſſed in the Engliſh language by the ſame vowels ; but alſo, in many particular words, a kind of ar-
bitrary

bitrary pronunciation is ufed, which cannot eafily be reduced to rule, and is therefore moft commonly taught merely by ear, or imitation.

This latter difficulty, I am afraid, cannot be removed; but, I think, it may be relieved in fome degree, by feparating all fuch words from thofe which are capable of being taught by rule. This I have attempted, and have accordingly collected all, or the greateft part of fuch kind of words, under their proper heads, as exceptions to the feveral rules given in the following pages, together with a fhort explanation of their found.—By this means a learner may have his tafk before him, and may eafily refer to any particular word, as he fhall have occafion; which will greatly relieve his memory.

I have not taken notice of all the derivatives and compounds which properly belong to the feveral exceptions, but for the moft part of primitive words only, for the fake of brevity; which I hope will be thought fufficient,

cient, the others being naturally comprehend-
ed therein. Many words indeed are varied
according to the different pofition of the accent, which not only fhortens the articulation of the fucceeding fyllables, but in fome
words caufes them to be fo indiftinctly pronounced, that it is fometimes difficult to determine what vowels are founded therein : yet
if the learner is but careful to give the accented fyllable its proper pronunciation according to the following rules, he will naturally fall into the cuftomary utterance of the
other fyllables, which, as they are pronounced
quick, need not be ftudied fo particularly.

The rules treat only of the general power
of the vowels and diphthongs, becaufe in thefe
confift the moft material differences between
the Englifh pronunciation and that of foreigners ; but I have added thereto, by way of ap-
pendix, a fhort treatife (drawn up and com-
municated by a friend) for the explanation
of fuch particularities alfo of the other letters
as are peculiar to the Englifh tongue.

All

All which together (I flatter myfelf) will be fufficient to enable a foreigner to read and pronounce any Englifh words with eafe and certainty, when the fyllables of the fame are properly divided according to the learned Dr. Lowth's excellent rule for fpelling, given in the 7th page of his Englifh grammar, viz. " The beft and *only fure rule* for dividing " the fyllables in fpelling, is to divide them " as they are naturally divided in a right " pronunciation ; without regard to the deri- " vation of words, or the poffible combina- " tion of confonants at the beginning of a " fyllable."

Mr. John Gignoux likewife particularly re-commends and explains this method, in the preface to his fpelling-book, intituled, " *The* " *Child's beft Inftructor in Spelling and Read-* " *ing.*" A title which it feems well to de-ferve, on account of the divifion of the feve-ral fyllables according to the manner above-mentioned, by which it is rendered (in my opinion at leaft) the moft ufeful book of the fort that has hitherto been publifhed.

I muft

I muft however obferve, that the author, in his " *Table of Words written very different* " *from their Pronunciation*," at page 82, has too much followed the common London pronunciation ; which, tho'. perhaps in general the beft, yet has fome very exceptionable particularities. Among which are, *Potticary* for Apothecary, *Athift* for Atheift, *Awkurd* for Aukward, *Riccolas* for Auricolas, *Belcony* for Balcony, *Carrin* for Carrion, *Sirket* for Circuit, *Growner* for Coroner, *Gorjus* for Gorgeous, *Hankerchur* for *Handkerchief*, *Purn* for Iron, *Ilan* for Ifland, *Spanel* for Spaniel, *Stummuch* for Stomach, *Sound* for Swoon, *Thufty* for Thirfty, *Vawt* for Vault, *Venzun* for Venifon, *Verdit* for Verdict, &c.

Alfo in page 57 he fignifies that the terminations -*tial*, -*cial*, -*cian*, -*tious*, -*cious*, -*tient*, and *cient*, make each of them " *but one found or* " *fyllable*." But however common fuch pronunciation may be, it ought not by any means to be taught, or laid down as a rule ; becaufe the Englifh language lofes much of its elegance,

gance, when it is expreſſed in ſo careleſs a manner, that any of the above-mentioned terminations ſhall ſeem but one ſyllable. . ..

The *i* in all theſe terminations has the ſound of the Engliſh *e* ; and though it is pronounced quick, yet it ought to be diſtinctly expreſſed, as in *Parti-al, Soci-al, Greci-an, Capti-ous, Graci-ous, Quoti-ent, Anci-ent,* &c. There fore I hope that the author, in his next edition of that uſeful book, will make ſome alteration in his explanation of theſe particulars.

Others, beſides Mr. Gignoux, have been miſled by the indiſtinct manner in which ſome particular ſyllables are ſometimes uttered even by good ſpeakers. Mr. James Buchanan in particular has given himſelf much unneceſſary trouble, and has carried his refinements a great deal too far concerning ſyllables of this kind, which, in quick pronunciation, have ſeemed to him to partake of an articulation different from the real ſpelling. This has, unfortunately, not only added great difficulty to

his

his * performance, but rendered it almoſt in-
capable of anſwering the good purpoſes in-
tended by it. For he has frequently ſubſtituted an imaginary articulation of one vowel
for the inarticulation, or rather the ſhort and
indiſtinct found, of another; not conſidering
that the expreſſing of an accented ſyllable in
many particular words does almoſt unavoid-
ably cauſe the ſucceeding ſyllable or ſyllables
to be ſo indiſtinctly pronounced, that it is
ſometimes difficult to determine what vowels
are founded therein, as I have before obſerved.

But when words are ſo pronounced, that in-
ſtead of the ſhort or indiſtinct found of one
vowel, a manifeſt articulation of another different vowel may be diſtinguiſhed; it then be-
comes a fault in ſpeech, which (howſoever
common it may be) ought by no means to be

* " An Eſſay towards eſtabliſhing a Standard for an ele-
" gant and uniform Pronunciation of the Engliſh Language,
" as practiſed by the moſt learned and polite Speakers."

imitated,

imitated, much lefs taught; becaufe the ge-nerality of people are naturally too liable of themfelves to acquire it, without being led thereto by written inftructions.

The following examples taken from Mr. Buchanan's book will illuftrate what has been faid; viz. He has fubftituted -ĭl for the ter-minations -al, -ial, and -el, as *Nắivĭl, Neu-trĭl, Kŏmĭk l, Joodĕĕſhĭl, Spĕ́ſhĭl, Quắrĭl,* &c. for Naval, Neutral, Comical, Judicial, Spe-cial, Quarrel, &c. * -*in* for -an, as *Heumin, Orgĭn,* &c. for Human, Organ, &c. -*ĭnſs* for -ance and -ence; and -*ĭnt* for -ant and -ent, as *Abundĭnſs, Rĕvĕrĭnſs, Contentmĭnt, Com-mandmĭnt,* &c. inftead of Abundance, Re-verence, Contentment, Commandment, &c.

---

* Mr. Peyton's " *New Vocabulary or Grammar of the true pronunciation of the Engliſh*" is not leſs liable to cen-fure, for the fame words are there rendered Nai-vel, Niou trel, djŏu-dĭ-chiel, Spe-chiel, Couâr-ril, &c.

-fŏol

-*fool* for -ful as *Faithfool*, &c. *ifs* for *efs*, as *Heedlifs*, *Hppinifs*, and a great abundance of fuch other fyllables, equally diftant from the true pronunciation.

As I have no other motive for giving my opinion fo freely concerning this gentleman's performance, than the defire of removing all unneceffary difficulty from the learning of Englifh, I hope he will excufe me; even though my remarks fhould not have fufficient weight to convince him.

He may likewife affure himfelf, that, though I think an uniformity of pronunciation through-out the Britifh dominions is more to be wifhed than hoped for; yet I fhould have as much real fatisfaction as himfelf in the completion of that " *great moral end*," which (as he fup-pofes in his preface) would be promoted thereby, viz. the removal of *national preju-dice*; an effect equally to be defired by all lovers of their country, whether South or North Britons!

It would be much to the advantage of all thofe who learn the Englifh tongue, if the

fyllables

fyllables in all future editions of Englifh dictionaries were divided according to the * method recommended by Dr. Lowth and Mr.
Gignoux before mentioned: and likewife if the
words, which are not properly Englifh, were
diftinguifhed by an afterifk, or fome other particular mark placed before them; that foreigners may not conceive our language to be un-
neceffarily copious and difficult.

The coining of new words from other languages to exprefs any thing, which might as
concifely and elegantly be explained in proper
Englifh words, is a kind of pedantry, which
all writers fhould endeavour to avoid: unlefs
we be allowed to except thofe who treat of na-
tural philofophy, medicine, furgery, or fuch
other fubjects as are fuppofed to be read by
none but thofe who are acquainted with other
languages, or at leaft have fome knowledge of

---

* A very ufeful little dictionary on this plan was printed
in 1764, for J. Nourfe and S. Hooper in the Strand,
intituled, " the Complete Englifh Spelling Dictionary
upon an entire new Plan ; " the author, Mr. J. Carter.

the

the Latin tongue. For it ought to be the ftudy of every writer to make his meaning as plain and intelligible in the proper language in which he writes, as he poffibly can. Yet fo many of our moft eminent writers have oc-cafionally been guilty of the fault above men-tioned, that the ingenious Mr. Johnfon has thought himfelf obliged to infert a great abun-dance of fuch coined words into his excellent Englifh dictionary; and the reverend Mr. Entick likewife into his very ufeful new pocket dictionary. But I cannot fuppofe that fuch kind of words were admitted by thefe gen-tlemen as proper Englifh words; but merely that they might explain them to Englifh rea-ders; who without the knowledge of other languages cannot otherwife poffibly understand them: which is a fufficient proof that they are not at all intitled to the name of Englifh words.

For how fhould an Englifh reader (I mean a reader merely of Englifh) be fuppofed to under-ftand that *Ablepfy* fignifies blindnefs? *Acetofity* fournefs? *Anhelation* panting? *Arcanum* a fecret?

fecret? *Obefity* fatnefs? *Papilio* a butterfly?
*Neoterick*, modern? *Paranymph* a bride-man?
*Rugofe* wrinkled? *Squalor* naftinefs? *Terreous*
earthy? *Tenebricofe* dark; *Tripudiation* dancing?
*Tumefy* to fwell? *Turm* a troop? and a thou-
fand other fuch words, which are found in
both dictionaries?

It is much to be wifhed that all fuch new
coined words, which have only been ufed by a
few authors, were diftinguifhed by fome mark
from the common and proper Englifh words
(as I have hinted above) in all future editions
of thefe ufeful dictionaries: left fo many un-
couth and pedantick expreffions fhould be
adopted into the Englifh tongue by dictionary
authority. Becaufe when a perfon fees them
ranged with other words in an Englifh dictionary, he may be induced to make ufe of
them as proper Englifh words in his writing
and difcourfe, which would, at firft, caufe no
fmall impediment to the underftanding of his
ordinary readers and hearers.

The

The accents ufed in thefe dictionaries are particularly ufeful for keeping up an uniformity in pronunciation; and it would be well if the double accents were alfo added to fome particular words, as in Mr. Gignoux's fpelling book for the purpofe mentioned in page 7 of his preface, viz. To denote, that " the confonant " that begins the next fyllable muft be alfo " founded at the end of the fyllable where " the double accent is; as a''-tóne-ment; " man''-gle; in-tan''-gle; which words muft " be founded as if written at-tone-ment; " mang-gle; intang-gle;" fo in con''-quer-or; con''-cu-bine; &c.*

In my fearch for fuch words as are independent of the following rules, I made ufe of the Rev. Mr. Entick's new fpelling dictionary; and though I examined the fame fo carefully,

---

* The fame would alfo be particularly ufeful in words, wherein g and c are foftened by the vowels e and i following them in the next fyllable as in neg-lig''-ent; vo-rac''ity, &c.

c                    that

that I believe I have not made many omiſſions,
yet the whole number of particular exceptions
(excluſive of their compounds and derivatives)
amount to no more than † 340—which number
bears a very ſmall proportion to the number
of words in that dictionary; which I compute
to be upwards of 23,000. This, I think,
ought to prove that the Engliſh pronunciation
is not ſo very irregular as it is generally thought
to be; which a careful examination of the following pages will more particularly ſhew.

---

† There are indeed 54 foreign words beſides; (ſee
page 15) which are not included in this number, becauſe,
as they ſtill retain their original pronunciation (or nearly
ſo) they cannot properly be accounted exceptions to
Engliſh rules.

A SHORT

# A SHORT

# TREATISE

## ON THE

# ENGLISH TONGUE.

---

**T**HE Englilh vowels, a, e, i, o and u, have each of them* 2 *founds*, commonly called *long* and *fhort*.
The founds of the three firft vowels a, e, and i, when long, feem to be peculiar at prefent to this nation, wherefore they may properly be called the Englilh founds.

---

* The vowels may indeed be faid to have more founds than 2, becaufe a different pronunciation from the 2 founds here fpoken of, is given to each of the vowels in a few particular cafes, which are hereafter noted; but at prefent I am only fpeaking of their general power.

And

And the short sounds of these three vowels may, for the sake of distinction, be called the foreign sounds; because they are uttered with scarcely any difference (except that a and i, are pronounced short) from the French articulation of the same vowels; which shall be more fully explained by * examples hereafter.

I think it neceſſary to obſerve in this place that the Engliſh ſound of the following vowels, diphthongs and terminations cannot eaſily be expreſſed in foreign letters, and ſhould therefore be learned by ear, viz.

i long †, as in Bi-ble, Mi-tre, Nitre, Pirate, &c.

---

* See the examples to the 2d rule.

† There are 2 ways of ſounding the long i and y (though both long) the one a little different from the other, and requiring a little more ex enſion of rhe mouth, as may be ſeen by compaiing the following words, viz. I and Aye, High and High-ho; By't (or by it) and Bite; Sigh'd and Side; Strive and Strife, &c. but this difference being ſo nice, is not to be attained but by much practice, neither is it very material.

o and

o and u fhort, before a confonant in the fame
   fyllable as in Odd, Nod, Lord,
   &c. and in Mud, Strut, Stun,
   Urn, &c.

oi and oy, which have both the fame found,
   as in Oil, Boil, Coil, Boy, Coy,
   Hoy, &c.

ou and ow (not like the French ou, in the
   pronunciation of which the lips
   are almoft clofed, but) with an
   open articulation as in Pound,
   Our, Gown, Pow-er, &c.

 Alfo the following Terminations, viz.

-ire ⎫
-tion ⎬ as in Dire, Fire, Salvation, Deli-
-cious ⎪ cious, Fictitious, &c.
-tious ⎭

The Englifh (or long) found is given to **Rule**
the vowels a, e, and i (and the other vowels **I.**
are alfo founded long) when they are alone,
or when there is not a confonant following
them in the fame fyllable (alfo before filent e
in the end of a word; fee the 3d rule)

        a like

Exam-
ples

a } like the } e in Bête, as in Ca-ble,
Fa-ble, Sa-ble, &c.
e } French } i in Mille, as in Be, He,
E-vil, Be-ver, Le-gal, &c.

i like the Greek * ει or something like the
French i long before n in *Divin*, *Prince*,
*Enfin*, &c. as in Bi-ble; Di-al; Fi-nal;
Gi-ant, &c.

o like the French o or au, as in Go; So;
Lo-cal; Mo-ment, &c.

u like ew in Few, Pew, &c. as in Du-ty,
Fu-ry, Hu-man, &c.

y (when a vowel) like the Englifh i; as in
the monofyllables Buy and Guy, (wherein u is mute) Dry, Fry, My, Dye, &c.
in the diffyllables, Ally', Com-ply',
De-ny', De-fcry', De-fy', Ef-py', Im-
ply', Re-ly', and Re-ply', which are accented on the ultimate fyllable; and in
all words compounded with the Latin
word Fio; as Dé-ify, Magnify, Spe-
cify, Rarify, &c.

* At quoties litera i longa eft plerumque effertur ut
Græcorum ει. See Wallis's Grammatica Linguæ An-
glicanæ.

(Par-

(Particular Exceptions concerning *a*, at the End of a Syllable)

Except, 1ft, } a in *Wa-ter*, wherein it is commonly pronounced like the French *a*, or Englifh diphthong *aw*; in *Fa-ther*, and the laft fyllable of *Pa-pa*, *Mam-ma*, wherein it has a medium found between *aw* and the Englifh a; and in *a-ny*, and *ma-ny*, wherein it founds like a fhort *e*.

(Particular Exceptions concerning *i*)

2dly, i in *ac-qui-efce*, *Bi-er*, *Pi-er*, and *Tier*, wherein it founds like the Englifh *e*.

(General Exceptions concerning *i*)

3dly, i is pronounced fhort before another vowel in the termination of all words of more than 2 fyllables, when it is not radical; as in *A'mi-able*, *De-mo-ni-ac'k*, *Ca'r-ri-age*, *So'-ci-al*, *Wi'l-li-am*, *Sty'g-i-an*, *Da'l-li-ance*, *Va'l-i-ant*, *Spän-i-ard*, *A'-pi-ary*, *So'-ci-ate*, *In-fid-ia'tor*, *Al-le-vi a'tion*, *Ma'r-ri-ed*, *A-li-en*, *Co'n-fci-ence*, *Am'-bi-ent*, *Gla-*

*Gla-zĭ-er, Spe'-cĭ-es, Se-rag''-lĭ-o, Ax'-i-om,
Poſ-te'-rĭ-or, Wa'r-rĭ-our, Con'-ſcĭ-ous, Pd-
ĭ-ot, Pre'-mĭ-um,* &c. But in the proper
names *Ma-r-i'a* and *So-ph-i'a*, when given to
Engliſh women, it is pronounced according to rule. Alſo, in *A'ffi'-ance,* and the
derivatives from the diſſyllables ending in
*y,* which are mentioned in the example:
as *Al-li'-ance, Com-pli'-ance, De-ni'-al, De-
fi'-ance,* and *Re-li'-ance,* wherein the *i* * retains the ſound of the *y* in the original
words, and is accented accordingly.

Particular Exceptions concerning o.

Except,
4thly, } o in *Do* (and its compounds) *To,* and
*Who,* which is commonly pronounced like
*oo*; though the latter (*Who*) is pro-

---

* When *i* is ſubſtituted for *y* in the terminations of
derivatives, it retains the ſound of the *y* in the original
word, whether long or ſhort; therefore *i* in *Cār-rĭ-er,
Cār-rĭ-ed,* and *Cār-rĭes,* is ſhort; and in *Al-lī-ance, De-
nī-al, Dig-ni-fī-ed, Im-plīes,* &c. is pronounced long
like the *y* in the primitive words before ſpecified.

nounced

nounced according to the rule in the northern parts of England.

5thly,   u, in the firſt ſyllable of *Cu-cumber*, which
is commonly pronounced like the Engliſh
*ou* hereafter explained.

General Exception concerning y.

6thly,   y, at the end of all words of two or more ſyllables (except thoſe mentioned in the example) is pronounced like a ſhort *i*, as in
*Carry*, *Envy*, *Commiſſary*, &c. the accent
being laid on one of the former ſyllables.

Of vowels in ſyllables ending with a conſonant.

Rule II.   The vowels are pronounced ſhort in all ſyllables ending with a conſonant (except in the
particular caſes hereafter noted) and the three
firſt vowels have the foreign articulation, without any other material difference, except that
of being pronounced ſhort.

B                    a has

EXAMPLES.

{
a has a ſhort articulation of the Engliſh *aw*, or rather of the Italian *a*, as in *Add, Bad, Lad, Mad*, &c.

e has exactly the ſound of the \* Italian or French *é*, as in *Bed, Fed, Led, Red*, &c.

i has a ſhort articulation of the † French *i*, or Engliſh *e*, as in *Bid, Did, Hid, Kid*, &c.

The ſhort ſound of the two other vowels (viz. *o* and *u*) muſt be acquired by ear, as I have before obſerved (ſee examples of theſe vowels in p. 3. of this treatiſe.)
}

## Particular Exceptions concerning *a* before a conſonant.

Except, 1ſt,

a in *An-gel, Baſs, Ca'm-brick, Ca'm-bridge, Da'n-ger,* and *Ma'n-ger,* is commonly ſounded like the French diphthong *ai*; in *han't* (for *have not*) *Ma'ſ-ter,* and *Pla'ſ-ter,* it

---

\* *Italos* ego, uti noſtros etiam recte eam (literam e) proferre cenſeo in vocibus, aſcendo, ventus, &c. (Dr. Middleton, fol. 446.)

† I vocalis, quoties brevis eſt, ſonatur plerumque (ut apud Gallos aliofque) exili ſono. Wallis, fo. 47.

has

has a medium found between *aw* and the Englifh *a*; and in *Hal-fer* (wherein *l* is mute) *Falfe*, and *Palfy*, it is commonly pronounced like *aw*.

General Exceptions concerning *a* before a confonant.

2dly, a˙ has the found of *aw* likewife before *ld* and *lt*, as in *Bald, Cal-dron, Altar*, &c.; in all primitive monofyllables ending in *ll* (except *fhall* and *Mall*, which are pronounced according to rule) as in *All, Gall, Fall*, &c.; and before *lk* (wherein *l* is mute) as *Balk, Stalk, Walk, Talk*, &c. : but before *lf, lm, lve,* and before *nd* in words derived from the Latin word *Mando*, it is founded like the Italian *a*, only fomewhat longer, as in *Half, Calm, Salve, Command, Demand*, &c.

Particular Exceptions concerning *e* before a confonant.

Except, 3dly, e in *England, Pretty, Yes*, and *Yet*, wherein it is pronounced like a fhort *i*, and in *Yellow* like a fhort *ă*.

General

General Exception concerning *e* before *s*.

4thly, *e* is pronounced long before * *s* in the ultimate of plural nouns, and third perfons
fingular of verbs when preceded by *c*, *s*,
*z*, or *g*, as in *Fa'-ces*, *Ho'r-fes*, *Af-fi'-zes*,
*Ra'-ges*, &c. ; but in all other terminations
with filent *e* (except in Latin words) the
*es* may be founded in the fame fyllable,
as *Bride Brides*, *Ride Rides*, *Name Names*,
&c.

Particular Exceptions concerning *i* before a
confonant.

5thly, *i* in *Blithe*, *Endict*, and *Indict* (wherein *c* is
mute) *Mild*, *Pint*, and *Wild*, retains its
Englifh, or long found ; alfo in *Child* and
*Chrift*, but not in their Derivatives, *Chil-
dren*, *Chriften*, and *Chriftian*.

---

* *S* final in thefe cafes is always pronounced like *z*.

General

General Exceptions concerning *i* before a confonant.

6thly, i is likewife founded long in all primitive
words (and their compounds and derivatives) ending in *nd*; as *Bind, Rind, Wind*,
&c.; though in *Wind*, the fubftantive, and
its compounds, it is fometimes pronounced
fhort.

It is alfo founded long before *gh*, as in
*High, Nigh, Light*, &c. in which *gh* is
mute, having no other ufe than that of
lengthening the *i*.

It is long alfo before *gn* at the end of a
word (and the *g* is mute) as in *Benign*,
*Sign*, and its compounds *Confign, Defign*,
&c. and their Derivatives in *-er, -ed, -edly*,
and *-ment*, but no others; for in *Re-fig-na-
tion, Con-fig-na-tion, Sig-nif-i-ed*, &c. the *i*
is fhort according to rule, and the *g* is pronounced.

General Exceptions concerning *o* before con-
ſonants.

Except,  o in all words ending in *ld* and *lt*, as *Beho'ld,*
7thly,      *Bold, Cold, Bolt, Colt,* &c. and all their
          compounds and derivatives, retains its long
          ſound.

    Particular Exceptions of *o* before a conſo-
    nant.

8thly,  o is alſo pronounced long in *Boll, Bolſter,*
        *Comb* (wherein *b* is mute) *Control, Droll,*
        *Folk* (wherein *l* is mute) *Force, Fort, Ghoſt,*
        *Groſs, Ho'lſter, Hoſt, Moſt, Only, Poſt,*
        *Poll, Pat-ro'll, Port, Roll, Scroll, Sloth,*
        *Sport,* and *Sword* (wherein *w* is mute)
        *Stroll, Toll,* and *Troll,* and in their com-
        pounds, &c. But in *Compt* and its com-
        pounds, *Ac-compt,* &c. it ſounds like the
        Engliſh diphthong *ou,* as if ſpelt *Count,*
        *Ac-count,* &c.

        It has the ſound of a ſhort *u* * in
        *Af-fro'nt, At-to'r-ney, Bomb, Bo'r-age,*

---

    * In the dialects of Lancaſhire, and ſome other places,
the *o* is pronounced according to rule, in many of theſe
words.

                                        *Bo'-rough,*

*Bo'r-ough, Bro'th-er, Co'l-our, Co'm-fits, Co'm-fort, Co'm-pany, Co'm-pafs, Co'n-duit, Co'n-ey, Co'n-fta-ble, Co'z-en, Co'v-e-nant, Cǒ'v-er, Co'v-et, Co'v-ey, Dif-co'm-fit, Do'z-en, Go'v-ern, Ho'n-ey, Lo'n-don, Mo'n-day, Mon-ey, Monk, Mo''n-key, Mo''n-ger, Mo''n-grel, Mo'nth, Mo'th-er, On-ion, O'th-er, O'v-en, Po'm-mel, Po'th-er, Ro'm-age, Ront, Son, Sho'v-el, Slo'v-en, Smo'th-er, Ton, Tho'r-ough-ly, Won, Wo'n-der, Word, World, Work, Worm, Wor-fted, Worth, Wo'm-an* (in the fingular only, the plural being pronounced as if fpelt *Wimmen*) *Wo'r-ry, Wort, Wo'r-fhip,* and their compounds, &c. except *Dif-co'v-er* and *Re-co'v-er,* which are pronounced according to rule.

It is moft commonly founded like *oo* in *Tomb* and *Womb* (wherein *b* is filent) *Lo-fer, Gold, Whom,* and *Whofe\* :* and is mute in *Jeo'p-ar-dy, Leo'p-ard,* and *Peo-*

---

\* In the northern parts of England the words *Gold, Who, Whom,* and *whofe,* are pronounced properly as they are fpelt.

*ple,*

*ple*, which are pronounced as if written *Jép-par-dy*, *Lep-pard*, and *Pee-ple*.

Particular Exceptions of *u* before a confonant.

Except, 9thly,
} u in *Bu-fy*, and its compounds, &c. which is commonly pronounced like a fhort *i*, and the *s* like *z*.

Of Vowels in Syllables ending with filent *e*.

Rule III.
But when *e* or *ue* follow a confonant in the fame fyllable, the preceding vowel retains its original open or long found.

EXAMPLES.
*Ace*, *Face*, *Recé'de*, *Dice*, *Vote*, *Con-fú'te*, *Vague*, *Vogue*, *Col-le'gue*, &c. Alfo, *Ad-vice*, *De-vi'ce*, *En-ti'ce*, *Suf-fi'ce*, *Sac-rif-i'ce*, *A-li've*, *Con-ni've*, *Con-tri've*, *De-pri've*, *De-ri've*, *Re-vi've*, and *Sur-vi've*, which are accented on the laft fyllable.

The vowel *a* is founded long even before *two confonants*, when they are followed by *e* in the fame fyllable (except before *-nce*) as in *Ache*, *Hafte*, *Wafte*, *Change*, *Grange*, *Range*, &c. and their compounds and derivatives ; but the other four vowels are

are founded fhort in the like cafe, as in *Fringe, Revenge, Solve, Serve, Tinge, Sludge, Grudge,* &c.

**Note,**

That derivatives from words ending in *e* for the moft part retain their original found, even when the *e* is omitted, as *Sparing, -ed,* from *Spare*; *Waft-er, -ing, ed,* from *Wafte*; *Rang-er, -ing, ed,* from *Range,* &c.

**Except, 1ft,**

### General Exception.

Words having the accent on the penultima or antepenultima: in all which the laft fyllable, being fhort, is pronounced as if the *e* and *ue* final were abfent, as in *Ca'la-mine, Ca'th-er-ine, Ca't-a-logue, De'c-alogue, De-po'f-ite, De'f-tine, De-te'r-mine, Dif-fra'n-chife, Do'c-trine, E'n-gine, E'pil-ogue, E'x-quif-ite, Gra'n-ite, Har-a'ngue, Fi'-nite,* and its compounds, *Ma'r-it-ime, Me'd-ic''-ine, Mi'n-ute* (not the adjective for *fmall*) *Mor-tife, Pe'd-a-gogue, Pra'c-tife* (verb) *Pro'l-ogue, Pro'm-ife, Sap''-phire, Syn'a-gogue, Tre'a-tife,* and *U-rine.*

C                                        Particular

## Particular Exceptions.

2dly,

The following monofyllables are likewife exceptions to this rule, viz. *Dare* (the verb) *Give*, *Gone*, *Have*, *Live*, and *One* *; all which

Except,

are pronounced as if *e* final was abfent.

3dly,

*There*, *Were*, and *Where*, which are commonly pronounced as if fpelt with the diphthong *ai*, *Thair*, *Wair*, and *Whair*; but in all other words (except what are mentioned above) the vowels *a*, *e*, *i*, or *y*, when they come before † -*re* final, are founded long according to the third rule, as in *Are*, *Care*, *Here*, *Mere*, *Defire*, *Fire*, *Lyre*, &c. as if fpelt *Air*, *Cair*, *Heer*, *Meer*, *Defier*, &c.

## Particular Exceptions concerning *i* in fyllables ending with filent *e*.

Except,

4thly,

*i*   in *Writhe* and *O-blige*, wherein it is commonly founded like *ee* (though in the

---

* *One* is pronounced as if fpelt *Won*.

† When a confonant comes before *re* and *le* final, the *e* is never founded laft, but always before the laft confonant of the word, as in *A-cre*, *Mi-tre*, *humble*, &c. which are founded *A-ker*, *Mi-ter*, *humbel*, &c.

northern

northern parts of England the latter is founded according to rule).

General Exceptions concerning *i* in syllables ending with silent *e*.

5thly,  i  in all adjectives of more than one sylla-ble ending in -*ile*, and in all words (except those mentioned in the above example) ending in *ice* and *ive*, is pronounced short, as in *Se'r-vile*, *Ju'-ven-ile*, *Ca'p-rice*, *Ma'l-ice*, *En'-dive*, *Po'f-it-ive*, &c.

Particular Exceptions concerning *o* in sylla-bles ending with silent *e*.

6thly,  o in *A-bo've*, *Come*, *Co'me-ly*, *Done*, *Dove*, *Glove*, *Love*, *Po're-blind*, *Some*, *Shove*, *Sponge*, *Tongue*, and *Worfe*, wherein it is founded like a short *u*; and in *Lofe*, *Move*, *Prove*, and *Rome*, wherein it is commonly pro-nounced like *oo*.

Of·

## Of Proper Diphthongs.

Proper Diphthongs have founds of their own, different from the long and fhort founds of the Englifh vowels.

Rule IV    *au* ⎫ are pronounced like the French *a* in
         *aw* ⎭    *Aine*.

Exam-
ples.       *Maul, Paul, Sprawl, Law, Saw &c.*

### Particular Exceptions.

Except,     *Auf* (more commonly fpelt *Oaf*) and *Hautboy*, wherein *au* is pronounced like a long *o* ; *Cauliflower*, where it is pronounced like a fhort *o* ; and *Gauge*, wherein it is commonly founded like the Englifh *a* long.

Rule V.   *oi* ⎫ The proper articulation of thefe diph-
         *oy* ⎭    thongs is that which is given them in the Englifh words *Oil, Boil, Coy, Hoy, &c. (See Lift of Vowels, Diphthongs, &c. which cannot be expreffed in foreign Letters, page 3.)*

2

Except,

Except,    *Tor-toife*, wherein *oi* is commonly founded like fhort *u*.

Rule VI  oo is pronounced like the French *ou* in *Bout*.

Examp*    *Boot, Broom, Loop, Moor, Poor,* &c.

Except,    *Blood, Flood, Foot, Good, Hood, Stood, Soot, Wood,* and *Wool,* wherein *oo* is not pronounced fo full, but partakes a little of the found of a fhort *u*. Except alfo * *Door* and *Floor,* wherein *oo* has the found of *o* long.

Rule VII.  ou } The proper pronunciation of thefe diph-
           ow }   thongs is that which is given them in the Englifh words *Bound, Found, Crown, Cow, Flow-er, Sow* (noun), *Coward,* &c. A more particular account of this found is given in page 3.

---

* *Door* and *Floor* are pronounced by the vulgar in the northern parts of England as they are fpelt; for they give the *oor*, in thefe words, the fame found that it has in *Boor, Moor, Poor,* &c.

Particular

Particular Exceptions concerning *ou*.

Except,

1ft,   ou in *Bou'ge, Bou'g-et* (commonly written *Budge* and *Budget*) *Bo'r-ough, Cou'n-try, Cou"-ple, Cou'r-age, Cou'f-in, Dou"-ble, Dou'b-let, Jou'r-nal, Jou'r-ney, Mounch, Nou'r-ifh, Tho'r-ough-ly, Tho'r-ough-fare, Trou"-ble, Touch,* \* *Scourge, Shou'd, Cou'd,* and *Wou'd,* wherein it is pronounced like a fhort *u*; alfo in *Enough, Rough, Slough* (when it fignifies the part which feparates from a fore) and *Tough*; in all which the *gh* final founds like *f*; but in *Cough, Lough* (or Lake) and *Trough*, it is pronounced like a fhort *o*, as if fpelt *Coff, Loff*, and *Troff.* Except alfo in *Coul-ter, Courfe,* (and its compounds *Difcourfe*, &c.) *Court, Dough, Four, Fur-lough, Gourd, Mourn, Mould, Moult, Poult, Poul-try, Poul-ter-er, Poul-tice, Shoul-der, Soul, Though,* wherein *ou* is founded like *o* long; and

---

\* *Ou* in *Scourge* is fometimes like *o* long.

like

like *oo* in *Boufe, Ca-roufe, Gouge, Through,* and *Un-couth.*

#### General Exceptions concerning *cu.*

Except, 2dly, ou before *ght*, which has a medium found between *aw* and *o* long, as in *Ought, Bought, Thought,* &c. and in the termination of words of more than one fyllable, in *-our* and *-ous*, wherein it founds like a fhort *u*, as in *Ho-nour, Sa-viour, Pi-ous, Righteous,* &c.

#### Particular Exceptions concerning *ow.*

Except, 3dly, ow in *Bow* when it fignifies a weapon, or fegment of a circle ; but in the word *Bow* it is pronounced according to rule ; in *Bowl* (or *Bafon,* not in *Bowl* the verb, nor its derivatives, &c.) *Blow, Crow, Flow, Flown* (from *Fly*) *Glow, Grow, Know, Low, Mow, Owe, Own, Prow, Prowl, Row, Sow* (the verb) *Show, Slow, Snow, Strow, Stow, Tow* (noun and verb) *Trow,* and *Throw,* and their derivatives, &c. wherein it founds like *o* long.

General

Except,     General Exception concerning *ow*.

4thly,     ow final in words of more than one fyllable, which is founded like a fhort *o*, the *w* being mute; as in *Ba'r-row*, *Be'llow*, *Fo'l-low*, &c. Three words are independent of this exception, viz. *Al-low*, wherein *ow* is pronounced according to the rule, and *Be-low* and *Beſtow*, wherein it founds like *o* long.

Note,     Many of the words contained in the above exceptions are pronounced in the broad dialects of the northern parts of England as they are fpelt; that is, *ou* and *ow* are pronounced according to the VIIth rule, as in *Bound*, *Cow*, &c. viz. *Trough* (making *gh* filent) *Four*, *Mould*, *Moult*, *Poultry*, *Poultice*, *Shoulder*, *Bowl* (or *Ba-ſon*) *Glow*, *Grow*, *Mow*, *Owe*, *Own*, *Strow*, *Trow*, *Ought*, *Bought*, &c.

Of Improper Diphthongs.

Improper Diphthongs take the found of but one of their vowels, the other being mute.

Rule

Rule VIII.
$$\left.\begin{array}{l} ai \\ ay \\ ey \end{array}\right\}$$ are pronounced like the French *ai*, or Englifh *a* long.

Exam-ples.

> *Dainty, Bail, Gain, Day, May, Grey, Prey, Convey, Obey, Survey, Bey, Dey,* &c.

Except, 1ft,

Particular Exceptions concerning *ai*.

ai in *Vil-lain* and *Mur-rain*, and fometimes in *Said*, is pronounced like a fhort *e*.

Except, 2dly,

General Exception concerning *ai*.

ai when alone or at the end of a fyllable, as in *A-chai-a*, and the Hebrew names *Ben-a'i-ah, If-a'i-ah, Mi-cai-ah, Cai-a-phas,* &c: wherein it is pronounced like the Greek α or *Englifh i* long.

Except, 3dly,

Particular Exceptions concerning *ey*.

ey in *Hey !* and *Hey-day !* wherein it is founded like the Englifh *i*, and in *Ceylon, Key,* and *Sey-mour,* wherein it is pronounced like the Englifh *e* or French *i*,

D

General

Except,

General Exception concerning *ey*.

4thly, ey at the end of words of more than one fyllable (when the accent is placed on a former fyllable, as in *A'l-ley*, *At-to'r-ney*, *B'arley*, *Ga'l-ley*, *Ho'n-ey*, &c.) is pronounced like a fhort *i*.

Rule
IX.

æ
ea
ee
ei
ie
œ

} are pronounced like the French *i* in *Fille*, or the Englifh *e* long.

Examples.

*Dæmon* (or *Demon*) *Beat*, *Dear*, *Lead*, and *Read* (verbs) *Meet*, *Feet*, *Re-ceipt*, *Deceit*, *De-ceive*, *Ceil-ing*, *Seign-iory*, *Seize*, *Shield*, *Re-prieve*, *Grief*, *Fœtus*, *Sub-pœna*, &c.

Except,
1ft,

Particular Exceptions concerning *ea*.

ea is pronounced like the French *é* in *Bread*, *Break-faft*, *Breaft*, *Breath* (noun only) *Cleanly*, and *Cleanfe* (not in *Clean*) *Dead*, *Deaf*,

*Deaf, Death, Dread, En-deav-our, Fea-ther, Head, He'av-en, He'av-y, Je'al-ous, Le'av-en, Lead* (metal) *Le'ath-er, Me'af-ure, Mif-tea'ch, Pea'f-ant, Phe'af-ant, Plea'f-ant, Ple'af-ure, Pea'f-cod, Read-y, Realm, Read* (only in preter tenfe and participle paffive) *Stead-y, In-ftead, Spread, Sweat, Teat, Thread, Threat-en, Trea'ch-ery, Tread, Tre'af-ure, Wea'th-er, Wea'p-on, Wreak, Zea'l-ous, Zeal-ot* (not in *Zeal*) *Yeaft,* and their compounds and derivatives not already excepted. But in *Bear* \*, *Break, Great, Swear, Tear* (the verb) *Wear, Wheal,* and *Weal* (the mark of a ftripe, but not in *Weal* for profperity) it is commonly founded like the French diphthong *ai* ; and like a fhort *a* in *Hear-ken, Hearth,* and *Heart.*

General Exceptions concerning *ea.*

Except, 2dly,

But in all other words before *r*, when another confonant follows in the fame fyl-

---

\* In the northern parts of *England, Break* and *Great* are pronounced according to rule.

D 2

lable,

lable, it is founded like *er* or *ir*, as in
*Dearth, Earl, Earn, Ea'rn-eft, Earl-y,
Earth, Hearfe, Heard, Learn,* &c.

ea before three confonants in the fame fyllable
is pronounced like the French é, as in
*Health, Breadth, Wealth,* &c.

Except,
3dly,

Particular Exceptions concerning *ee*.

ee in *Breech* (noun and verb) *Breechings,* and
*Breeches,* which are pronounced like a
fhort *i*.

Except,
4thly,

Particular Exceptions concerning *ei*.

ei in *Sleight (Artifice)* in which it is pronounced like the long Englifh *i* ; but it is
like a fhort *i* in *Fo'r-feit* and *Su'r-feit* ; like
a fhort *e* in *For-eign,* and *Hei-fer* ; and like
the diphthong *ai* in *Hei'n-ous, Heir, Leif-
ure* (though fometimes like a fhort *e* in
*Lei'f-ure) Skein, Their, Veil,* and *Vein.*

Except,
5thly,

General Exceptions concerning *ei*.

ei is pronounced like the long Englifh *i* when
it is not followed by a confonant in the

3                                    fame

same syllable; as in *Plei'-a-des*, *Hei'-del-berg*; *Hei-den-heym*, *Rei-gate*, &c. but in *ei-ther* and *nei-ther* it is sometimes pronounced like the English *a* long, and sometimes according to rule, like the English *e* long.

It has the sound of the English *a* in all words wherein it precedes -*gh*, *gn*, and -*nt* in the same syllable, as *Weigh*, *Freight*, *Deign*, *Feign*, &c. (in all which *g* is mute) *Feint*, *Teint*, &c. except in three words mentioned above, viz. *Sleight*, *Seignory*, and *Foreign*.

Particular Exceptions concerning *ie*.

Except, 6thly, ie in *Friend*, wherein it sounds like a short *e*; and *Sieve*, wherein it sounds like a short *i*.

General Exceptions concerning *ie* and *oe*.

7thly, ie } at the end of a word are always pronounced like the first vowel in each diphthong, viz. *ie* like *i* long, and *oe* like *o* long, as in *Die*, *Foe*, &c. except in two words, *Shoe* and *Ca'n-oe*, wherein *oe* is commonly pronounced like *oo*.

Note,

Note,     The same is to be observed of the diphthongs *ue* and *ye*, at the end of a word ;
the former being pronounced like a long
*u*, and the latter like a long *i* ; as in *Due,*
*Pye*, &c. the same likewise when *s* is added
to make the plural of nouns, or third person
singular of verbs, as *Dies, Foes, Dues, Pyes,*
&c. and the *s* so added is pronounced like *z.*

Rule X.  -eu
       -ew } are sounded like a single *u* long.
       -iew

    Examples. *Europe, Eu-nuch, Brew, Dew,*
    *View*, &c.

Except*, ew in *Sew*, which is commonly sounded like
    a long *o.*

Rule XI oa is pronounced like *o* long.
    Examples. *Boat, Coat, Groan, Moan*, &c.

Except,     in *Broad, A-broad*, and *Groat*, wherein
it partakes a little of the sound of *aw* ;
and in *Goal* (when it signifies a prison) it

---

* Eau in *Beauty* (and its derivatives) has likewise the
same sound.

                                    sounds

founds like *ai*, and the G is pronounced foft, as if fpelt *Jail*.

Rule XII.    ue } ui } before a confonant in the fame fyllable have the fhort found of the laft vowel in each diphthong ; viz. *ue* like a fhort *e* as in *Guefs, Gueft*, &c. ; and *ui* like a fhort *i*, as in *Build, Guild, Conduit*, &c. But in words ending with filent *e*, the diphthong *ui* is pronounced like the Englifh *i* long, according to the third rule, as in *Guide, Guile, Difguife*, &c.

Except, 1ft,

#### Particular Exceptions.

The following words, wherein the *u* alone is pronounced, viz. *Bruife, Cruife, Fruit, Juice, Nui-fance, Pur-fuit, Re-cruit, Sluice, Suit*, and *Suit-or*, which are founded as if fpelt *Bruze, Cruze, Nu-fance*, &c.

Note,

When *ua, ue, ui*, and *uo* follow Q in the fame fyllable, the *u* has the power of *w*, which power cannot more eafily be ex-plained to foreigners, than by comparing it to the found of *u* in the French word *Quoi !* or *Quoy !* as in *Qua'r-rel, Quack, Queftion, Quick, Quite, Quit, Quote*, &c.

A T A B L E of Words which are independent of the foregoing Rules and Exceptions, with the common Pronunciation of
each expreſſed in Italicks.

BUOY *Boey*, Victuals *Vittles*, Colonel
*Curnel*, George *Jorge*, Lieutenant *Leuf-
tenant*, Quay *Kee*, Two *Too*, Yacht *Yot*, Yeo-
man *Yewman*, Yelk or Yolk (of an egg) *Yoke*.

---

A T A B L E of Foreign Words which
ſtill retain their original Pronunciation (or
nearly ſo) notwithſtanding that they are in
a manner adopted, by frequent Uſe, into
the Engliſh Language.

ACcoutre, Antique, Archives, Arriere,
Banditti, Beau, Bureau, Caviare, Car-
touch, Connoiſſeur, Courier, Croup, Cuiraſs,
Environ, Eſcritoire, Faſcine, Groupe, In-
trigue, Lieu, Machine, Magazine, Marine,
Palanquin, Pas, Piquant, Pique, Piquet, Po-
lice, Poltron, Ponton, Prame, Profile, Ren-
dezvous, Roquelaure, Rouge, Scout, Sophi,
Soup, Tête-à-tête, Tornado, Toupee, Tour,
Tranſmarine, Vermicelli, Violoncello, Jonquil,
Adieu.

F I N I S.

# A TABLE or INDEX of the Words, which (with their ſeveral Compounds and Derivatives) are Exceptions to the foregoing Rules ; *viz.*

## A

| | | Vowels. | Sounded like | Rule. | Exception. | Page. |
|---|---|---|---|---|---|---|
| A-Bo've | — *Au-deſſus* — | o | ŭ | 3 | 6 | 17 |
| A-bro'ad | — *Dehors* — | oa | aw | 11 | 1 | 28 |
| Ac-qui-e'ſce | — *Acquieſcer* — | i | ē | 1 | 3 | 5 |
| Af-fro'nt | — *Affront* — | o | ē ŭ | 2 | 8 | 12 |
| An'-gel | — *Ange* — | a | ̄ā ē | 2 | 1 | 8 |
| A'-ny | — *Aucun* — | a | ē ē ŭ | 2 | 1 | 5 |
| At-to'r-ney | — *Procureur* — | o | ē ŭ ŭ | 2 | 8 | 12 |
| Auf | — *Sot* — | au | ō | 4 | 1 | 18 |

## B

| | | Vowels. | Sounded like | Rule. | Exception. | Page. |
|---|---|---|---|---|---|---|
| Baſs | — *Baſſe* — | a | ā | 2 | 1 | 8 |
| Bear (noun & verb) | *Ours* et *Supporter* | ea | ai | 9 | 1 | 25 |
| Be-lo'w | — *En-bas* — | ow ⎰ | ō | 7 | 4 | 22 |
| Be-ſto'w | — *Donner* — | ow ⎱ | | | | |
| Bi'-er | — *Une Biére* — | i | ē | 1 | 2 | 5 |
| Blith | — *Joyeux* — | i | ī | 2 | 5 | 10 |
| Blood | — *Sang* — | oo | ŭ | 6 | 1 | 19 |
| Blow | — *Coup, Souffler* — | ow | ō | 7 | 3 | 21 |
| Boll | — *Tige* — | o | ō | 2 | 8 | 12 |
| Bol-ſter | — *Chevet* — | o | ō | 2 | 8 | 12 |
| Bomb | — *Bombe* — | o | ō ŭ | 2 | 8 | 12 |
| Bo'r-age | — *Bourache* — | o | ŭ | 2 | 8 | 12 |
| Bor-ough | — *Bourg* — | o | ŭ ⎰ | 2 | 8 | 13 |
| | | | ⎱ | 7 | 1 | 20 |
| Bouge | — *S'enfler* — | ou | ŭ | 7 | 1 | 20 |
| Bou'g-et | — *Bougette* — | ou | ŭ | 7 | 1 | 20 |
| Bouſe | — *Boire avec excés* | ou | oo | 7 | 1 | 21 |
| Bow (noun) | — *Arc* — ⎰ | ow | ō | 7 | 3 | 21 |
| Bowl (or Baſin) | *Baſſin* — ⎱ | | | | | |

Bread

| | | Vowels | Sounded like | Rule. | Excepⁿ | Page. |
|---|---|---|---|---|---|---|
| Bread — | *Pain* — | ea | ě | 9 | 1 | 24 |
| Break ——— | *Rompre* — | ea | ā | 9 | 1 | 25 |
| Break-faſt — | *Déjeuné* — | ea | | | | |
| B-eaſt — | *Poitrine* — | ea | ě | 9 | 1 | 24 |
| Breath (noun) | *Haleine* — | ea | | | | |
| Bree'ch, -es, -ings | *Feſſes, Culotte* — | ee | ĭ | 9 | 3 | 26 |
| Broad ——— | *Large* — | oa | aw | 11 | 1 | 28 |
| Bro'th-er ——— | *Frere* — | o | ŭ | 2 | 8 | 13 |
| Bruiſe ——— | *Contuſion* — | ui | ū | 12 | 1 | 29 |
| Bu'ſy — | *Occupé* ——— | u | ĭ | 2 | 9 | 14 |

## C

| | | Vowels | Sounded like | Rule. | Excepⁿ | Page. |
|---|---|---|---|---|---|---|
| Cam-brick — | *Batiſte* ——— | a | ā | 2 | 1 | 8 |
| Cam-bridge — | *Cambridge* — | a | ā | 2 | 1 | 8 |
| Can-o'e ——— | *Canoe* ——— | oe | oo | 9 | 7 | 27 |
| Car-ou'ſe — | *Faire la débauche* | ou | ∞ | 7 | 1 | 21 |
| Cau'-lif-lower — | *Choux-fleur* — | au | ŏ | 4 | 1 | 18 |
| Cey'-lon ——— | *Ceylon* ——— | ey | ē | 8 | 3 | 23 |
| Child { but not their } | *Enfant* } | i | ī | 2 | 5 | 10 |
| Chriſt { deriva-tives. } | *Chriſt* } | | | | | |
| Clean-ly } not in { | *Propre* } | ea | ě | 9 | 1 | 24 |
| Cleanſe } clean { | *Nettoyer* } | | | | | |
| Co'l-our ——— | *Couleur* ——— | o | ŭ | 2 | 8 | 13 |
| Comb ——— | *Peigne* ——— | o | ō | 2 | 8 | 12 |
| Come ——— | *Venir* ——— | o | ŭ | | | |
| Come-ly ——— | *(De bonne grace)* | o | ŭ } | 3 | 6 | 17 |
| Comfits ——— | *Confitures* —. | o | ŭ | 2 | 8 | 13 |
| Com-fort — | *Conſolation* — | o | ŭ | 2 | 8 | 13 |
| Com-pany — | *Compagnie* — | o | ŭ | 2 | 8 | 13 |
| Com-paſs — | *Contour* — | o | ŭ | 2 | 8 | 13 |
| Compt — | *Compte* ——— | o | ou | 2 | 8 | 12 |
| Con-duit — | *Conduit* ——. | o | ŭ | 2 | 8 | 13 |
| Con-ey — | *Lapin* ——— | o | ŭ | 2 | 8 | 13 |

Con-ſta-ble

| | | Vowels | Sounded like | Rule. | Excep<sup>n</sup> | Page. |
|---|---|---|---|---|---|---|


| | | Vowels | Sound-ed like | Rule. | Excep<sup>n</sup> | Page. |
|---|---|---|---|---|---|---|
| Con-fta-ble { | (Commiffaire de quartier) } | o | ŭ | 2 | 8 | 13 |
| Con-trol — | Controller (laft fyl.) | o | ō ŭ | 2 | 8 | 12 |
| Cou'd — | (Verbe) — | ou | ŭ | 7 | 1 | 20 |
| Cov-en-ant — | Accord — } | | | | | |
| Cov-er — | Couverture — } | o | ŭ | 2 | 8 | 13 |
| Cov-et — | Convoiter — } | | | | | |
| Cov-ey ——— | Volée d'oifeaux } | | | | | |
| Cough — | Toux ——— | ou | ŏ | 7 | 1 | 20 |
| Coul-ter — | (Soc de charrüe) | ou | ō | 7 | 1 | 20 |
| Coun-try — | Pays — } | | | | | |
| Cou-ple — | Couple — } | ou | ŭ | 7 | 1 | 20 |
| Cour age — | Courage — } | | | | | |
| Courfe (Dif-courfe, &c.) } | Cours — } | ou | ō | 7 | 1 | 20 |
| Court — } | Cour — } | | | | | |
| Cou'f-in — | Coufin — | ou | ŭ | 7 | 1 | 20 |
| Coz-en (verb) | Duper — | o | ŭ | 2 | 8 | 13 |
| Crow ——— | Corneille — | ow | ō | 7 | 3 | 21 |
| Cruife — | Croifer — | ui | ū | 12 | 1 | 29 |
| Cu'-cum-ber { | Co'ncombre (1ft fyll.) } | u | ou | 1 | 5 | 7 |

### D

| | | | | | | |
|---|---|---|---|---|---|---|
| Da'n-ger — | Danger — | a | ā | 2 | 1 | 8 |
| Dare — | Ofer — | a | ă | 3 | 2 | 16 |
| Dead — | Mort — | ea | ĕ | 9 | 1 | 24 |
| Deaf — | Sourd — | ea | ĕ | 9 | 1 | 24 |
| Death — | La mort — | ea | ĕ | 9 | 1 | 24 |
| Difcomfit — | Défaire — | o | ŭ | 2 | 8 | 13 |
| Do — | Faire — | o | oo | 1 | 4 | 6 |
| Done — | Fait — | o | ŭ | 3 | 6 | 17 |
| Door — | Porte — | oo | ō | 6 | 1 | 19 |
| Dove — | Colombe — | o | ŭ | 3 | 6 | 17 |

E 2                                   Dou"ble

| | | Vowels | Sounded like | Rule | Exceptⁿ | Page |
|---|---|---|---|---|---|---|
| Dou''-ble — Doubler — | | ou | ŭ | 7 | 1 | 20 |
| Doub-let — Doublet — | | | | | | |
| Dough — Pâte — | | ou | ōŭ | 7 | 1 | 20 |
| Doz-en — Douzaine — | | o | ōŭĕ | 2 | 8 | 13 |
| Dread — Crainte — | | ea | ŭĕ | 9 | 1 | 24 |
| Droll — Comique — | | o | ō | 2 | 8 | 12 |

**E**

| | | Vowels | Sounded like | Rule | Exceptⁿ | Page |
|---|---|---|---|---|---|---|
| En-de'av-our — Effort — | | ea | ĕ | 9 | 1 | 25 |
| En-dict & Indict Stiler — | | i | īĭ | 2 | 5 | 10 |
| Eng-land — Angleterre — | | e | ĭ | 2 | 3 | 9 |
| En-ou'gh — Assez — | | ou | ŭ | 7 | 1 | 20 |

**F**

| | | Vowels | Sounded like | Rule | Exceptⁿ | Page |
|---|---|---|---|---|---|---|
| False — Faux — | | a | au | 2 | 1 | 9 |
| Fa'-ther — Pere — | | a | aw | 1 | 1 | 5 |
| Fea'-ther — Plume — | | ea | ĕŭ | 9 | 1 | 25 |
| Flood — Deluge — | | oo | ŭ | 6 | 1 | 19 |
| Floor — Plancher — | | oo | ō | 6 | 1 | 19 |
| Flow — Couler — | | ow | ō | 7 | 3 | 21 |
| Flown (from Fly) Echapé — | | ow | ō | 7 | 3 | 21 |
| Folk — Gens — | | o | ō | 2 | 8 | 12 |
| Foot — Pied — | | oo | ŭ | 6 | 1 | 19 |
| Force — Force — | | o | ō | 2 | 8 | 12 |
| Fort — Fort — | | o | ō | 2 | 8 | 12 |
| Fo'r-eign — Etranger — | | ei | ĕ | 9 | 4 | 26 |
| | | | | 9 | 5 | 27 |
| Fo'r-feit — Amende — | | ei | ĭ | 9 | 4 | 26 |
| Four — Quatre — | | ou | ō | 7 | 1 | 20 |
| Friend — Ami — | | ie | ĕ | 9 | 6 | 27 |
| Fruit — Fruit — | | ui | ū | 12 | 1 | 29 |
| Fu'r-lough — Congé — | | ou | ō | 7 | 1 | 20 |

Gauge

|  |  | Vowels | Sounded like | Rule. | Exception. | Page. |
|---|---|---|---|---|---|---|
| **G** |  |  |  |  |  |  |
| Gauge | Jauge | au | ā ō | 4 | 1 | 18 |
| Ghost | Esprit | o | ō | 2 | 8 | 12 |
| Give | Donner | i | ĭ | 3 | 2 | 16 |
| Glove | Gand | o | ŭ | 3 | 6 | 17 |
| Glow | (Etre allumé) | ow | ō | 7 | 3 | 21 |
| Goal | Prison (G soft) | oa | ā | 11 | 1 | 28 |
| Gold | Or | o | oo | 2 | 8 | 13 |
| Gone | Allé | o | ŏ | 3 | 2 | 16 |
| Good | Bon | oo | ŭ | 6 | 1 | 16 |
| Go'v-ern | Gouverner | o | ŭ | 2 | 8 | 13 |
| Gouge | Gouge | ou | oo | 7 | 1 | 21 |
| Gourd | Citrouille | ou | ō | 7 | 1 | 20 |
| Great | Grand | ea | ā | 9 | 1 | 25 |
| Groat | (Piece de 4 sols) | oa | aw | 11 | 1 | 28 |
| Gross | Gros | o | ō | 2 | 8 | 12 |
| Grow | Croitre | ou | ō | 7 | 3 | 21 |
| **H** |  |  |  |  |  |  |
| Ha'l-ser | Haussiere (l mute) | a | aw | 2 | 1 | 9 |
| Han't (for have not) | (Verbe) | a | aw | 2 | 1 | 8 |
| Have | Avoir | a | ā | 3 | 2 | 16 |
| Hau't-boy | Hautbois (t mute) | au | ō | 4 | 1 | 18 |
| Head | Tête | ea | ĕ | 9 | 1 | 25 |
| Hea'r-ken | Ecouter | ea | ā | 9 | 1 | 25 |
| Heart | Cœur | ea | ā | 9 | 1 | 25 |
| Hearth | Foyer | ea | ā | 9 | 1 | 25 |
| Hea'v-en | Le ciel | ea | ĕ | 9 | 1 | 25 |
| Heav-y | Pésant | ea | ĕ | 9 | 1 | 25 |
| Hei'f-er | Géniffe | ei | ĕ | 9 | 4 | 26 |
| Hei'n-ous | Odieux | ei | ā | 9 | 4 | 26 |
| Heir | Heritier (h mute) | ei | ā | 9 | 4 | 26 |
| Hey! He'y-day! | Ouais! | ey | ī | 8 | 3 | 23 |

| | | Vowels | Sound-ed like | Rule. | Excepⁱ | Page. |
|---|---|---|---|---|---|---|
| Ho'l-ſter — { | (Fourreau de piſtolet — } | o | ō | 2 | 8 | 12 |
| Hon-ey — | Miel — | o | ŭ | 2 | 8 | 13 |
| Hood — | Coiffe — | oo | ŭŭ | 6 | 1 | 19 |
| Hoſt — | Hôte — | o | ō | 2 | 8 | 12 |

**I**

| | | Vowels | Sound-ed like | Rule. | Excepⁱ | Page. |
|---|---|---|---|---|---|---|
| Jea'l-ous — | Jaloux — | ea | ĕ | 9 | 1 | 25 |
| Jeop-ard-y — | Peril — | eo | ĕ | 2 | 8 | 13 |
| In-ſtead — | Au lieu — | ea | ĕ | 9 | 1 | 25 |
| Journal — | Journal — } | ou | ŭ | 7 | ɼ | 20 |
| Jour-ney — | Voïage — } | | | | | |
| Juice — | Jus — | ui | ū | 12 | 1 | 29 |

**K**

| | | Vowels | Sound-ed like | Rule. | Excepⁱ | Page. |
|---|---|---|---|---|---|---|
| Key — | Clef — | ey | ee | 8 | ·3 | 23 |
| Know — | Sçavoir — | ow | ō | 7 | 3 | 21 |

**L**

| | | Vowels | Sound-ed like | Rule. | Excepⁱ | Page. |
|---|---|---|---|---|---|---|
| Lead (noun) — | Plomb — | ea | ĕ | 9 | 1 | 25 |
| Lea'th-er — | Cuir — | ea | ĕ | 9 | 1 | 25 |
| Lea'v-en — | Levain — | ea | ĕ | 9 | 1 | 25 |
| Lei'ſ-ure — | Loiſir — | ei | { ā and ſome-times ĕ } | 9 | 4 | 26 |
| Leo'l-pard — | Leopard — | eo | ĕ | 2 | 8 | 13 |
| Live — | Vivre — | i | ĭ | 3 | 2 | 16 |
| Lo'n-don — | Londres — | o | ŭ | 2 | 8 | 13 |
| Loſe, -er — | Perdant — | o | oo | 3 / 2 | 6 / 8 | 17 / 13 |
| Love — | Amour — | o | ŭ | 3 | 6 | 17 |

Lough

| | | | Vowels | Sounded like | Rule. | Excep. | Page. |
|---|---|---|---|---|---|---|---|
| Lough (or Lake) | Lac | — | o | ŏ ō | 7 | 1 | 20 |
| Low | — Bas | — | ow | ō | 7 | 3 | 21 |

### M

| | | | | | | | |
|---|---|---|---|---|---|---|---|
| Ma-ma' | — Maman | — | a | aw | 1 | 1 | 5 |
| Ma'n-ger | — Mangeoire | — | a | ā | 2 | 1 | 8 |
| Ma'-ny | — Plufieurs | — | a | ĕ | 1 | 1 | 5 |
| Ma'f-ter | — Maître | — | a | aw | 2 | 1 | 8 |
| Mea'f-ure | — Mefure | — | ea | ĕ | 9 | 1 | 25 |
| Mild | — Doux | — | i | ī | 2 | 5 | 10 |
| Mif-tea'ch | — Enfeigner mal | — | ea | ē | 9 | 1 | 25 |
| Mo'n-day | — Lundi | — | o | ŭ | 2 | 8 | 13 |
| Mo'n-ey | — L'argent | — | o | ŭ | 2 | 8 | 13 |
| -Mon-ger | — Vendeur | — | o | ŭ | 2 | 8 | 13 |
| Mon''-grel | — Métif | — | o | ŭ | 2 | 8 | 13 |
| Monk | — Moine | — | o | ŭ | 2 | 8 | 13 |
| Mon''-key | — Singe | — | o | ŭ | 2 | 8 | 13 |
| Month | — Mois | — | o | ŭ | 2 | 8 | 13 |
| Moft | — Le plus, la plus, &c. | o | ō ŭ | 2 | 8 | 12 |
| Mo'th-er | — Mére | — | o | ō ŭ | 2 | 8 | 13 |
| Move | — Mouvoir | — | o | oo | 3 | 6 | 17 |
| Mould | — Moule | — | ou | ō | 7 | 1 | 20 |
| Moult | — Muer | — | ou | ō | 7 | 1 | 20 |
| Mounch | — Manger | — | ou | ŭ | 7 | 1 | 20 |
| Mourn | — Deplorer | — | ou | ō | 7 | 1 | 20 |
| Mow | — Faucher | — | ow | ō | 7 | 3 | 21 |
| Mu'r-rain | Mortalité parmi les bêtes | ai | ĕ | 8 | 1 | 23 |

### N

| | | | | | | | |
|---|---|---|---|---|---|---|---|
| Nou'-rifh | — Nourrir | — | ou | ŭ | 7 | 1 | 20 |

Nuif-ance

| | | Vowels | Sounded like | Rule | Excepⁿ | Page |
|---|---|---|---|---|---|---|
| Nui′ſ-ance — | *Incommodité* — | ui | ū | 12 | 1 | 29 |

## O

| | | | | | | |
|---|---|---|---|---|---|---|
| O-bli′ge — | *Obliger (ſometimes)* | i | ee | 3 | 4 | 16 |
| One — | *Un, une* — | o | ŏ | 3 | 2 | 16 |
| On′-ion — | *Oignon (1ſt ſyll.)* | o | ŭ | 2 | 8 | 13 |
| On′-ly — | *Seul (ſometimes)* | o | ō | 2 | 8 | 12 |
| O′th-er — | *Autre* — | o | ŭ | 2 | 8 | 13 |
| Ov-en — | *Four* — | o | ŭ | 2 | 8 | 13 |
| Owe, Own — | *Devoir, confeſſer* | ow | ō | 7 | 3 | 21 |

## P

| | | | | | | |
|---|---|---|---|---|---|---|
| Pa′l-ſey — | *Paralyſie* — | a | aw | 2 | 1 | 9 |
| Pa-pa′ — | *Papa* — | a | aw | 1 | 1 | 5 |
| Pa-tro′l — | *Patrouille* — | o | ō | 2 | 8 | 12 |
| Pea′ſ-ant — | *Payſan* | ea | ĕ | 9 | 1 | 25 |
| Pea′ſ-cod — | *(Coſſe de pois)* | | | | | |
| Peo′-ple — | *Peuple* — | eo | ē | 2 | 8 | 13 |
| Phea′ſ-ant — | *Faiſand* — | ea | ē ĕ | 9 | 1 | 25 |
| Pi-er — | *Jettée* — | i | ē | 1 | 2 | 5 |
| Pint — | *Chopine* — | i | ī | 2 | 5 | 10 |
| Pla′ſ-ter — | *Emplâtre* — | a | aw | 2 | 1 | 8 |
| Plea′ſ-ant — | *Agréable* — | ea | ĕ | 9 | 1 | 25 |
| Plea′ſ-ure — | *Plaiſir* — | | | | | |
| Poll — | *Tête* — | | | | | |
| Port — | *Port* — | o | ō | 2 | 8 | 12 |
| Poſt — | *Poſte* — | | | | | |
| Po′m-mel — | *Pommeau* — | o | ŭ | 2 | 8 | 13 |
| Po′th-er — | *Embarras* — | | | | | |
| Po′re-blind — | *(qui a la vue courte)* | o | ŭ | 3 | 6 | 17 |
| Poult — | *Coup de main* | | | | | |
| Poul-try, Pou′l-ter-er — | *Volaille, Pou-lailler* — | ou | ō | 7 | 1 | 20 |

| | | Vowels | Sound-ed like | Rule. | Excepⁿ | Page. |
|---|---|---|---|---|---|---|
| Pou'l-tice — | Cataplâme — | ou | ō ĭ | 7 | 1 | 20 |
| Pre't-ty — | Joli — | e | ĭ | 2 | 3 | 9 |
| Prove — | Prouver — | o | oo | 3 | 6 | 17 |
| Prow — | Proüe — | ow | ō | 7 | 3 | 21 |
| Prowl — | Roder — | | | | | |
| Pur-sui't —— | Pourſuite — | ui | ū | 12 | 1 | 29 |

### R

| | | Vowels | Sound-ed like | Rule. | Excepⁿ | Page. |
|---|---|---|---|---|---|---|
| Read (perfect tenſe, parti-ciple paſſive) | Lû — | ea | ĕ | 9 | 1 | 25 |
| Rea'd-y — | Prêt — | ea | ĕ | 9 | 1 | 25 |
| Realm — | Royaume —— | ea | ĕ | 9 | 1 | 25 |
| Re-cruit —— | Recrüe —— | ui | ū | 12 | 1 | 29 |
| Roll — | Un rouleau — | o | ō | 2 | 8 | 12 |
| Ro'm-age — | Perquiſition — | o | ŭ | 2 | 8 | 13 |
| Rome — | Rome — | o | oo | 3 | 6 | 17 |
| Ront — | Animal nain — | o | ŭ | 2 | 8 | 13 |
| Rough — | Rude — | ou | ŭ | 7 | 1 | 20 |
| Row, noun & verb | Rang, ramer — | ow | ō | 7 | 3 | 21 |

### S

| | | Vowels | Sound-ed like | Rule. | Excepⁿ | Page. |
|---|---|---|---|---|---|---|
| Said — | Dit — | ai | ĕ | 8 | 1 | 23 |
| Scourge —— | Fleau — | ou | ŭ & ō | 7 | 1 | 20 |
| Scro'll — | Une bande —— | o | ō | 2 | 8 | 12 |
| Sew — | Coudre — | ew | ō | 10 | 1 | 28 |
| Sey-mour — | Sey-mour (nom) | ey | ē | 8 | 3 | 23 |
| Shoe — | Un ſoulier — | oe | oo | 9 | 7 | 27 |
| Shou'd — | (Verbe) — | ou | ŭ | 7 | 1 | 20 |
| Shove — | Pouſſer — | o | ŭ | 3 | 6 | 17 |
| Shov-el —— | Une péle — | o | ŭ | 2 | 8 | 13 |
| Shou'l-der — | Epaule — | ou | ō | 7 | 1 | 20 |
| Show — | Montrer — | ow | ō | 7 | 3 | 21 |

F

Sieve

| | | Vowels | Sound-ed like | Rule. | Excep' | Page. |
|---|---|---|---|---|---|---|
| Sieve — | *Crible* — | ie | ĭ | 9 | 6 | 27 |
| Skein — | *Echeveau* — | ei | ai | 9 | 4 | 26 |
| Sleight (Artifice) | *Artifice* — | ei | ī | 9 | 4 | 26 |
| | | | | 9 | 5 | 27 |
| Sloth — | *Pareſſe* — | o | ō | 2 | 8 | 12 |
| Slough (Suppuration from a ſore) | *Matiere qui ſort d'une playe* | ou | ŭ | 7 | 1 | 20 |
| Slo'v-en — | *Mal-propre* — | o | ŭ | 2 | 8 | 13 |
| Slow — | *Lent* — | ow | ō | 7 | 3 | 21 |
| Siuice — | *Ecluſe* — | ui | ū | 12 | 1 | 29 |
| Smo'th-er — | *Etouffer* — | o | ŭ | 2 | 8 | 13 |
| Snow — | *Neige* — | ow | ō | 7 | 3 | 21 |
| Some — | *Quelque* — | o | ŭ | 3 | 6 | 17 |
| Son — | *Fils* — | o | ŭ | 2 | 8 | 13 |
| Soot — | *Suie* — | òo | ŭ | 6 | 1 | 19 |
| Soul — | *Ame* — | ou | ō | 7 | 1 | 20 |
| Sow (verb) — | *Semer* — | ow | ō | 7 | 1 | 20 |
| Sponge — | *Epònge* — | o | ŭ | 3 | 6 | 17 |
| Sport — | *Jeu* — | o | ō | 2 | 8 | 12 |
| Spread — | *Étendre* — | ea | ĕ | 9 | 1 | 25 |
| Stea'd-y — | *Ferme* — | ea | ĕ | 9 | 1 | 25 |
| Stood — | *(Pret. de s'arreter)* | oo | ŭ | 6 | 1 | 19 |
| Stow — | *Arranger* — | ow | ō | 7 | 3 | 21 |
| Stroll — | *Roder* — | o | ō | 2 | 8 | 12 |
| Strow — | *Parſemer* — | ow | ō | 7 | 3 | 21 |
| Suit — | *Procés* — | ui | ū | 12 | 1 | 29 |
| Suit-or — | *Plaideur* — | ui | ū | 12 | 1 | 29 |
| Sur-feit — | *Indigeſtion* — | ei | ĭ | 9 | 4 | 26 |
| Swear — | *Jurer* — | ea | ai | 9 | 1 | 25 |
| Sweat — | *Suer* — | ea | ĕ | 9 | 1 | 25 |
| Sword — | *Epèe* — | o | ō | 2 | 8 | 12 |

### T

| Tear (verb) — | *Déchirer* — | ea | ai | 1 | 9 | 25 |
| Teat — | *Mammelle* — | ea | ĕ | 1 | 9 | 25 |

Ti-er

| | | Vowels | Sounded like | Rule | Excepⁿ | Page |
|---|---|---|---|---|---|---|
| Ti-er — | Rang — | i | ē | 1 | 2 | 5 |
| Their —— | Leur — | ei | ai | 9 | 4 | 26 |
| There — | Là — | e | ai | 3 | 3 | 16 |
| Though —— | Quoique — | ou | ō | 7 | 1 | 20 |
| Tho'r-ough-fare, Pa∬age, par- } | faitement —} | o | ŭ ŭ ĕ | 2 | 8 | 13 |
| Tho'rough-ly | | ou | | 7 | 1 | 20 |
| Thread —— | Fil — | ea | ĕ | 9 | 1 | 25 |
| Threa't-en — | Menacer — | ea | ĕ | 9 | 1 | 25 |
| Through — | à travers — | ou | oo | 7 | 1 | 21 |
| Throw — | Jetter —— | ow | ōŭ | 7 | 3 | 21 |
| To — | à —— | o | ŭ | 1 | 4 | 6 |
| Toll — | Péage — | o | ō | 2 | 8 | 12 |
| Tomb — | Tombeau — | o | oo | 2 | 8 | 13 |
| Ton — | Tonneau — | o | ŭ | 2 | 8 | 13 |
| To'ngue — | Langue — | o | ŭ ŭ | 3 | 6 | 17 |
| To'r-toife — | Tortüe — | oi | ŭ ŭ | 5 | 1 | 19 |
| Touch — | Toucher — | ou | ŭ ŭ | 7 | 1 | 20 |
| Tough — | Dur — | ou | ŭ | 7 | 1 | 20 |
| Tow, noun & verb | Etoupes, remorquer | ow | ō | 7 | 3 | 21 |
| Trea'ch-er-y — | Perfidie — | ea | ĕ ĕ ĕ | 9 | 1 | 25 |
| Tread —— | Marcher — | ea | ĕ ĕ | 9 | 1 | 25 |
| Trea'∬-ure — | Tréfor — | ea | ĕ | 9 | 1 | 25 |
| Tro'll — | Roder — | o | ōŭ | 2 | 8 | 12 |
| Trou'-ble — | Peine — | ou | ŭ | 7 | 1 | 20 |
| Trough —— | Auge — | ou | ŏ | 7 | 1 | 20 |
| Trow — | Croire —• | ow | ō | 7 | 3 | 21 |
| | **V** | | | | | |
| Veil — | Voile — | ei | ai | 9 | 4 | 26 |
| Vein —— | Veine — | ei | ai | 9 | 4 | 26 |
| Vi'l-lain — | Coquin — | ai | ĕ | 8 | 1 | 23 |
| Un-cou'th — | Gro∬er — | ou | o | 7 | 1 | |
| | **W** | | | | | |
| Wa'-ter — | L'eau — | a | aw | 1 | 1 | 5 |
| Weal (mark of a ftripe — } | Marque de coup | ea | āi | 9 | 1 | 25 |

F 2

Wea'p-on

| | | Vowels | Sound-ed like | Rule. | Excepⁿ | Page. |
|---|---|---|---|---|---|---|
| Wea'p-on — | Arme — | ea | ĕ | 9 | 1 | 25 |
| Wea'th-er — | Le tems — | ea | ĕ | 9 | 1 | 25 |
| Wear — | User — | ea | ai | 9 | 1 | 25 |
| Were — | (Être) — | e | ai | 3 | 3 | 16 |
| Wheal (a stripe) | Marque de coup | ea | ai | 9 | 1 | 25 |
| Where — | Où — | e | ai | 3 | 3 | 16 |
| Who — { | Qui, lequelle, laquelle — } | o | sometimes oo | 1 | 4 | 6 |
| Whom — | Lequelle, laquelle } | o | Dᵒ | 2 | 8 | 13 |
| Whose — | Dont — } | | | | | |
| Wild — | Sauvage — | i | ī | 2 | 5 | 10 |
| Womb — | Matrice — | o | oo | 2 | 8 | 13 |
| Wom'an, wom'en | Femme, -s — | o | ŭ | 2 | 8 | 13 |
| Won — | Gagné — | o | ŭ | 2 | 8 | 13 |
| Won-der — | Surprise. — | o | ŭ | 2 | 8 | 13 |
| Wood — | Bois — } | oo | ŭ | 6 | 1 | 19 |
| Wool — | Laine — } | | | | | |
| Word — | Mot — } | o | ŭ | 2 | 8 | 13 |
| World — | Monde — } | | | | | |
| Work — | Ouvrage — } | o | ŭ | 2 | 8 | 13 |
| Worm — | Ver — } | | | | | |
| Wo'rs-t d | Etame — } | | | | | |
| Wo'r-ry — | Dechirer — } | o | ŭ | 2 | 8 | 13 |
| Wo'r-ship — | Adoration — } | | | | | |
| Wort — | Moût — } | | | | | |
| Worth — | Prix — } | | | | | |
| Worse — | Pire — | o | ŭ | 2 | 8 | 13 |
| Wou'd — | (Verbe) — | ou | ŭ | 7 | 1 | 20 |
| Wreak — | Assouvir sa venge | ea | ĕ | 9 | 1 | 25 |
| Writhe — | Guirlande, tordre | i | ee | 3 | 4 | 16 |
| **Y** | | | | | | |
| Yeast — | Levure — | ea | ĕ | 9 | 1 | 25 |
| Ye'l-low — | Jaune — | e | ă | 2 | 3 | 9 |
| Yes — | Oui — } | e | ĭ | 2 | 3 | 9 |
| Yet — | Encore — } | | | | | |
| **Z** | | | | | | |
| Zea'l ous, Zea'lot | Zelé, zelateur — | ea | ĕ | 9 | 1 | 25 |

1

---

# A N

# APPENDIX,

### CONTAINING

A Brief Account of the chief Peculiarities
of the Enɢʟɪsʜ CONSONANTS.

1. *B* is mute before *t*, or after *m*, in the same
syllable, as *Debt*, *Lamb*, &c.

2. *C* sounds soft, like *s*, when followed by *e*, *i*, or
an apostrophe (denoting the absence of *e*)
as *Cedar*, *City*, *Danc'd*, &c.

*C* sounds like *sh*, when followed by *ea*, *ia*, *ie*,
or *io*, making different syllables, as *Ocean*,
*Ancient*, *Precious*, *Social*, &c. except *Society*.

*CC* when

*CC* when followed by *e* or *i*, founds like *x*, as *Accept*, *Accident*, &c.

*C* is mute in *Indict*, *Victuals*, *Scene*, *Scent*, *Science*, *Sciatica*, *Sciſſors*, *Sciſſion*, *Scymiter*, *Scythe*, and the proper names *Scyros*, *Scylla*, and *Scythia*.

 In all other caſes *C* founds hard like *k*.

3. *Ch*, when properly Engliſh, has the ſame found with the Italian *c*, before *e* or *i*. Examp. *Child*, *Chain*, &c.

 It founds alſo like *ſh*, in words derived from the French, as *Chaiſe*, *Champaigne*, &c. and like *k* in words of Greek extraction, as *Chriſt*, *School*, *Stomach*, *Archangel*, &c. pronounced *Ark-angel*. But if *Arch* comes before a confonant, *ch* has then its proper Engliſh found, as in *Archbiſhop*.

*Ch* in *Loch* founds like *f*.

*Ch* is mute in *Drachm*, *Schedule*, and *Schiſin*.

4. *D* is mute before *ge*, as in *Judge*, *Bridge*, &c. alſo in *Soldier*.

5. *F* in *Of* founds like *v*.

6.  *G* founds *foft* like *j* before *e*, *i*, or an *apoftro-phe*, and *hard* (like the Greek γ) in all other cafes.

Examp. *Angel, Rage, Rag'd, Giant, Ginger,* &c.

### Exceptions to *G*'s founding foft.

1. In the participles paffive of words ending in *g hard* (and alfo where-ever *g* is doubled) it continues hard, notwithftanding the vowels *e* or *i*, or an apoftrophe, as in *Dragg'd, Begging, Digging,* &c.

2. In the termination *ger*, where-ever it makes a diftinct fyllable, *g* founds hard, as in *An"-ger, Fin"ger, Lon"ger, Stron"ger,* &c. in which kind of words it may be ob-ferved that the *g* founds double, fo as to belong to both fyllables.

3. Derivatives in *er*, *ed*, or *ing* from primitives in *ng*, retain the *g* hard, as *Sing-ing, Sing-er,* from *Sing*; *Hang-ing, Hang-er,* from *Hang*; *Winged* or *Wing'd* from *Wing,* &c. In which kind of words it

may

may be obferved, that *g* founds *fingle;* and belongs to the *firft fyllable only.*

4. In the following words *G* is hard, notwithftanding it comes before *e* or *i* ; viz. *Geefe, Gewgaw, Geld, Gelt, Gertrude, Get* (with its compounds) *Gibberifh, Gibbous, Giddy, Gift, Gig, Giggle, Gild, Girl, Give, Forgive, Gilt, Gimblet, Gimp, Gird, Girt, Girdle, Begin, Gizzard, Gideon, Gibbons, Gilbert,* and *Gilpin.*

*G* is mute before *n* in the fame fyllable, as *Gnafh, Sign, Sovereign,* &c. alfo in *Phlegm, Seraglio,* and *Bagnio.*

7. *Gh* founds like *G hard* in *Ghoft,* and like *ff* in *Cough, Lough, Lough, Laughter, Rough, Slough, Tough, Trough,* and *Enough.* In other words it is mute.

8. *H* is mute in *Hour, Honour, Honeft, Heir, Herb, Humour, Hoftler, Thyme, John, Thomas, Thomafin,* and *Thames.* Alfo in Greek words, when preceded by *R,* as *Rheum, Rhyme, Rhetoric, Myrrh,* &c. and laftly at the end of words, as *ah, hah, Ifaiah, Sarah,* &c.

2                                    9. K

9. *K* is mute before *n* in the fame fyllable, as *Knave, Know, Knight,* &c.

10. *L* is mute in *Balk, Talk, Walk, Stalk, Balm, Calm, Calf, Calves, Falcon, Half, Halves, Holme* (an ifland) and *Holmes* (a furname) *Pfalm, Qualm, Salmon, Could, Should,* and *Would.*

11. *N* is mute after *m* in the fame fyllable, as *Hymn, Autumn, Solemn,* &c.

12. *P* is mute before *s,* and between *m* and *t,* as *Pfalm, Tempt,* &c.

13. *Ph* is always founded like *f,* except in *Stephen, Nephew,* and *Phial,* where it founds like *v.*

   *Ph* is mute in *Phthific,* and is pronounced *Tizzic.*

14. *Q* is always followed by *u,* and, when it begins a fyllable, founds like *cw,* by which (as Mr. Johnfon obferves) our Saxon anceftors well expreffed it. But in terminations from the Latin *-quus,* and alfo in words of French extraction, it founds like *k.* Examp. *Oblique, Antique, Quoif, Conquer, Rifque, Traffique,* &c. fome of which words

G                                          are

are now more commonly fpelt with *c* or *k*, as *Coif, Rifk, Traffic,* &c.

15. *S* founds like z.

> 1ft, In the third perfons fingular of all verbs, and the plural number of all nouns, as in *Has, Was, Tries, Bees, Times,* &c.

> 2dly, In pronouns poffeffive, as *His, Hers, Theirs,* and alfo when preceded by the comma denoting poffeffion, as *Father's, Mother's, Tom's, Will's,* &c. (alfo in the particle *as.*)

Exception to the two laft Sections.

*S* has its proper found when preceded by *c, k, ck, f, p, q,* or *t,* which admit not the found of z fo eafily after them, as *Speaks, Beats, Rocks, Jack's, Dick's, Gilbert's, Cock's-fpur, Cat's-paw,* &c.

> 3dly, *S* founds like z preceded by a liquid in the fame fyllable, as *Dam-fel, Crim-fon, Thames, Jer-fey, Guern-fey,* &c. And alfo,

4thly,

4thly, *S* between two vowels moſt commonly ſounds like *z*, as *Daiſy*, *Repriſal*, *Peaſant*, *Pleaſe*, *Roſin*, &c.

Except *Houſe*, *Mouſe*, *Louſe*, *Gooſe*, *Geeſe*, *Sauſage*, *Purchaſe*, *Promiſe*, *Caſe*, *Maſon*, *Baſon*, *Baſis*, *Phaſis*, and *Theſis*: Except alſo ſubſtantives in *uſe*, derived from Latin verbs, as *U'ſe*, *Abu'ſe*, *Diſu'ſe*, *Re'fuſe*, *Excu'ſe*, &c. and adjectives derived from the participles paſſive of ſome Latin verbs, as *Reclu'ſe*, *Profu'ſe*, *Abſtru'ſe*, &c.

Laſtly, Except alſo the words contained in the next ſection but one, where *s* ſounds like *zh*.

*S* and *ſs* ſound like *ſh* in *Sure* (with its compounds) *Iſſue*, *Tiſſue*, *Fiſſure*, *Preſſure*, *Ruſſian*, &c. alſo in the terminations -*aſſion*, -*eſſion*, -*iſſion*, -*uſſion*, as in *Paſſion*, *Impreſſion*, *Miſſion*, *Concuſſion*, &c.

*S*, when preceded by a vowel and followed by *ion* or *ian*, ſounds like *zh*, as *Invaſion*, *Epheſian*, *Viſion*, *Deluſion*, &c. But if it

G 2                                              be

be preceded by a confonant, it founds like *ſh*, as in *Converſion*, *Perſian*, &c.

*S* founds alſo like *zh* before *-ier*, as *Oſier*, *Hoſier*, *Glaſier*, *Braſier*, &c. and in the words *Leiſure*, *Meaſure*, *Pleaſure*, and *Treaſure*.

*S* is mute in *Iſle*, *Liſle*, *Carliſle*, *Iſland*, *Viſcount*, and *Demeſne*.

16.    *T* before *io* or *ia* (making part of the ſame ſyllable with *i*) founds like *ſh*, as *Na-tion*, *Cau-tious*, *Egyp-tian*, *Sa-ti-ate*, &c. But if *t* belong to the former ſyllable, it retains its proper Sound, as *Queſt-ion*, *Fuſt-ian*, *Combuſt-ion*, &c.

   *T* is mute in words ending with *-ſtle*, as *Caſtle*, *Thiſtle*, *Briſtle*, &c.

17.    *Th* has two founds, the one ſoft, as in *Thy*, the other hard (like the Greek Ϥ) as in *Thigh*.

I.    *Th* founds ſoft,

       1ſt, In *Thence*, *There* (with their compounds) *Then*, *That*, *The*, *Thee*, *Theſe*, *This*, *Thoſe*, *Thus*, *Thou*, *Thy*, *Thine*, *Their*, *Theirs*, *Them*, *Though*, *Although*, *Beneath*, *Bequeath*, *Betroth*, *Mouths*, *Tythe*, *Scythe*, *Wreath*, *Booth*, and in the

the verbs *Bathe, Mouth, Seeth, Loathe, Soothe,* and *Breathe.*

2dly, Where-ever it occurs between two vowels, as *Father, Mother,* &c. Except words of Greek extraction, and also derivatives from words ending with *th* hard, as *Earthen* from *Earth,* &c.

3dly, *Th* founds foft when placed between *r* and a vowel, as *Burthen, Murther,* &c. though in fuch words *d* is often written and pronounced inftead of *th,* as *Murder, Burden.* In other cafes *th* founds *hard.*

*Th* is mute in *Afthma,* with its derivatives.

18, *W* is mute before *r* in the fame fyllable, as *Write, Wrath,* &c. alfo in *Sword, Swoon,* and *Anfwer,* with their compounds and derivatives.

The other confonants have the fame powers as in other languages.

F I N I S.

# E R R A T A.

Preface, p. xiv. for 340, read 342.
———— Note, for 54 r. 47.
—— for page 15, r. page 30.
Page 21, for word, r. verb.

www.ingramcontent.com/pod-product-compliance
Lightning Source LLC
Chambersburg PA
CBHW022017080426
42733CB00007B/629